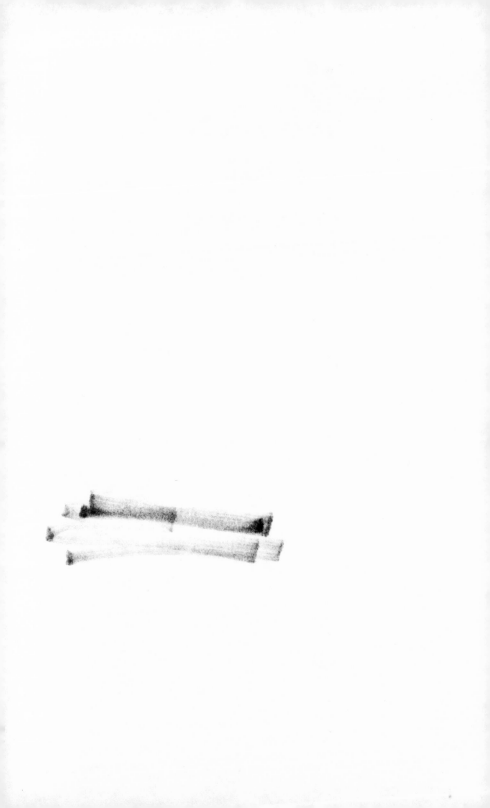

SKINS
AND
BONES

Paula Gunn Allen

Books by Paula Gunn Allen

Poetry:

The Blind Lion
Coyote's Daylight Trip
Star Child
A Cannon Between My Knees
Shadow Country
Wyrds

Fiction:

The Woman Who Owned the Shadows

Academic Writing:

Studies in American Indian Literature:
    Critical Essays and Course Designs (ed.)
The Sacred Hoop:
    Recovering the Feminine in American Indian Traditions

SKINS
AND
BONES

Poems 1979–87

Paula Gunn Allen

WEST END PRESS

Some of these poems have appeared in *The Creative Woman, Feminary, Open Mind, Songs from This Earth on Turtle's Back, Contact II, Frontiers, Calyx, A Gathering of Spirit, Backbone, 1983 Lunar Calendar, Parnassus, A Nation Within, That's What She Said, Star Child, What Cloud Threw This Light* and *The Harper's Anthology of Contemporary Native American Poetry.*

ISBN 0-931122-50-3

TABLE OF CONTENTS

TO AGNES GUNN GOTTLIEB: 1896–1985

In celebration of our lives and our deaths

ONE

C'koy'u, Old Woman
Songs of Tradition

C'KOY'U, OLD WOMAN

old woman there in the earth
outside you we wait
do you dream of birth, bring
what is outside   inside?

          old
              woman inside
                 old
                     woman outside

                 old woman there in the sky
                 we are waiting inside you
                 dreaming your dream of birthing
                 get what is inside/outside

          a hey a hey a hey a ho
          a hey a hey a hey a ho
          a hi oh ho a hi oh ho
          a hey a hey a hey a ho

EVE THE FOX

Eve the fox swung
her hips appetizingly, she
sauntered over to Adam the hunk
who was twiddling his toes and
devising an elaborate scheme
for renaming the beasts: Adam
was bored, but not Eve for she
knew the joy of swivelhips
and the taste of honey on her lips.
She was serpent wise and snake foolish,
and she knew all the tricks of the trade
that foxy lady, and she used them
to wile away the time: bite into this,
my hunky mate, she said, bending
tantalizingly low so her warm breasts
hung like peaches in the air. You
will know a thing or two when I get
through to you, she said, and gazed
deep with promise into his squinted eyes.
She admired the glisten of sweat and light
on his ropey arms, that hunky man of mine,
she sighed inside and wiggled deliciously
while he bit deep into the white fleshy
fruit she held to his lips. And wham-bam,
the change arose, it rose up in Adam
as it had in Eve and let me tell you
right then they knew all
they ever wanted to know about knowing,
and he discovered the perfect curve of her
breasts, the sweet gentle halfmoon of her belly,
the perfect valentine of her vulva,
the rose that curled within the garden
of her loins, that he would enter like bees,
and she discovered the tender power
of his sweat, the strong center of his
muscled arms, she worshipped the dark hair

that fell over his chest in waves.
And together riding the current of this
altogether new knowing they had found,
they bit and chewed, bit and chewed.

MALINALLI, LA MALINCHE, TO CORTÉS, CONQUISTADOR

And among other gifts of tribute the now-subdued people of the Maya coast gave to Cortés their choicest girls, and among these the slave-girl, Malinal. . . .

It was in March 1519 that the people of Tabasco gave the Lady Marina (as Bernal Diaz always speaks of her) to the strangers, and this was in the shadowland country at the far frontier of the Aztec confederacy. . . .

Throughout the first march on Mexico, after they were joined by Malinal, the Spanish were forced to fight in only one instance. . . . Otherwise the road of their first penetration into the country . . . was paved by a string of diplomatic victories as remarkable as so many straight passes at dice.

—William Brandon

Ever I twisted you to my will,
oh great bringer of the goddess' wrath,
for you did not know that she sang
of your victories before your name was dreamed,
before your flesh was formed.
Ah, you marched, brazen and satisfied,
certain of your cunning and your strength,
and of your place before all of the gods,
straight for the heart of my chief enemy,
he who gave his life and gold in fear,
but in certain knowledge of his part:
only you, unblessed conqueror,
father of my son, remained ignorant,
boastful of a power you would never own.
You stride the continents of your fool's pride
not knowing why it is I, Malinche, whose figure
looms large above the tales of your conquests.

The Spaniard has a disease for which
the only cure is gold, you said; nor
did you know the disease was more of the spirit
than of the flesh: you thought to mock
the piety of him who bowed before you,

of him who was my enemy, my companion,
my beloved Moctezuma. He gave you
all the gold you sought, unprotesting.
Did you ever think to wonder why?
Or how it could be that you,
paltry in your barbaric splendor,
alone could ride
across the jungles and the hills
to the heart of Áztlan?
Did you never wonder who it was
that led you in, let you in?
Did you never wonder why?

And I myself have been maligned: a fitting
irony. Maligned I, La Malinche,
chief of traitors, chief of slaves.
Betrayed I the father gods,
the false serpent who claimed
wings, who flew against
the grandmother sun declaring
prior right; who brought
murder and destruction, gold and jade;
who dreamed of war as tribute
for his blood-drenched kings.
And knowing this, still
I prayed to the mother of us all,
she of sun and star who gives
both life and light,
anguished did I pray to the serpent
woman who lies coiled and still, waiting.

The hour is late, Cortés.
And just as I stood
and watched you strip great
Moctezuma of his gold, just as I stood
guiding your words and your soldiers
with my gaze as I had guided them

with my many-flavored tongue,
I now stand, silent, still,
and watch with great Cihuacoatl
as your time runs out.
Listen: in the barrios even now I hear
her wailing cry as it was heard
in the chambers of the ruler a cycle ago:
oh, my beloved children,
where will I hide you?
Look into the holy mirror that you stole
from him, who you murdered for his will:
see if in its depth you can see my face,
glimpse the falling feathers
of your dying king.

POCAHONTAS TO HER ENGLISH HUSBAND, JOHN ROLFE

In a way, then, Pocahontas was a kind of traitor to her people. . . .
Perhaps I am being a little too hard on her. The crucial point, it seems
to me, is to remember that Pocahontas was a hostage. Would she have
converted freely to Christianity if she had not been in captivity? There
is no easy answer to this question other than to note that once she
was free to do what she wanted, she avoided her own people like the
plague. . . .

Pocahontas was a white dream—a dream of cultural superiority.

—Charles Larson
American Indian Fiction

Had I not cradled you in my arms
oh beloved perfidious one,
you would have died.
And how many times did I pluck you
from certain death in the wilderness—
my world through which you stumbled
as though blind?
Had I not set you tasks
your masters far across the sea
would have abandoned you—
did abandon you, as many times
they left you
to reap the harvest of their lies.
Still you survived, oh my fair husband,
and brought them gold
wrung from a harvest I taught you
to plant. Tobacco.
It is not without irony that by this crop
your descendants die, for other
powers than you know
take part in this and all things.
And indeed I did rescue you—
not once but a thousand thousand times
and in my arms you slept, a foolish child,
and under my protecting gaze you played,

8

chattering nonsense about a God
you had not wit to name.   I'm sure
you wondered at my silence, saying I was
a simple wanton, a savage maid,
dusky daughter of heathen sires
who cartwheeled naked through the muddy towns
who would learn the ways of grace only
by your firm guidance, through
your husbandly rule:
no doubt, no doubt.
I spoke little, you said.
And you listened less,
but played with your gaudy dreams
and sent ponderous missives to the throne
striving thereby to curry favor
with your king.
I saw you well. I
understood your ploys and still
protected you, going so far as to die
in your keeping—a wasting,
putrefying Christian death—and you,
deceiver, whiteman, father of my son,
survived, reaping wealth greater
than any you had ever dreamed
from what I taught you and
from the wasting of my bones.

MOLLY BRANT, IROQUOIS MATRON, SPEAKS

I was, Sir, born of Indian parents, and lived while a child among those whom you are pleased to call savages; I was afterwards sent to live among the white people, and educated at one of your schools; and after every exertion to divest myself of prejudice, I am obliged to give my opinion in favor of my own people. . . . In the government you call civilized, the happiness of the people is constantly sacrificed to the splendor of empire. . . .

—Joseph Brant

We knew it was the end
long after it had ended,
my brother Joseph and I.
We were so simple then,
taking a holiday to see the war,
the one they would later call
the Revolution.
The shot sent 'round the world
was fired from the Iroquois gun; we
could not foresee its round
would lodge itself
in our breast. The fury we unleashed
in pursuit of the Great Peace
washed the Mothers away,
our Lodges burned,
our fields salted,
our Ancient fires extinguished—
no, not put out, fanned,
the flames spread far
beyond our anticipation
out of control.
We had not counted on their hate;
we had not recognized
the depth of their contempt.
How could we know I would be
no longer honored matron
but heathen squaw—

in their eyes, my beloved daughters
half-breed dirt. Along with our earth
they salted our hearts
so nothing would grow
for too long a time.
We had been arrogant
and unwise: engaged in spreading
the White Roots of Peace, we
all but forgot the little ones
dear to our Mothers
and their ancestry,
the tender fortunes
of squash, corn and beans.

Then, overnight, was I
fleeing for my life
across the new borders, my brother hunted
like a common criminal
to be tried for sedition
for his part
among the British. They
lost out just as we'd planned
a century before. But
we had forgotten the Elder's Plan.
So it was we could not know
a Council Fire would be out,
the League unable to meet
in the bitter winter that fell
upon us like the soldiers
and the missionaries,
the carrion birds that flew
upon the winds of Revolution
to feed upon our scarred and frozen flesh.
We had not counted on fate—
so far from the Roots of our being
had we flown,
carried on the wings of an Algonquin priest

we fell into the eyrie
of a carrion host.
Perhaps it is the Immortals alone who know
what turns the Revolution must entail,
what dreams to send to lead us on,
far beyond the borders of our Dreams.
The turning of centuries goes on,
revolving along some obscure path
no human woman's ever seen.

That's how it is with revolutions.
Wheels turn. So do planets.
Stars turn. So do galaxies.
Mortals see only this lifetime
or that. How could we know,
bound to the borders we called home,
the Revolution we conspired for
would turn us under
like last year's crop?

I speak now because I know
the Revolution has not let up.
Others like my brother and like me
conspire with other dreams,
argue whether or not
to blow earth up, or poison it mortally
or settle for alteration. They
believe, like we, that the sacred fire
is theirs to control, but may be
this Revolution is the plan of gods,
of beings Matrons and priests alike
cannot know.

Still, let them obliterate it, I say.
What do I care? What have I to lose,
having lost all I loved so long ago?
Aliens, aliens everywhere,

and so few of the People
left to dream. All that is left
is not so precious after all—
great cities, piling drifting clouds
of burning death, waters that last drew breath
decades, perhaps centuries ago,
four-leggeds, wingeds, reptiles all
drowned in bloodred rivers of an alien dream
of progress. Progress is what
they call it. I call it cemetery,
charnel house, soul sickness,
artificial mockery
of what we called life.

I, Matron of the Longhouse, say:
If their death is in the fire's wind,
let it wash our Mother clean.
If Revolution is to take another turn,
who's to say
which side will turn up next?
Maybe when the last great blast goes up
you will hear me screaming with glee,
wildly drunk at last on vindication,
trilling ecstatically my longed-for revenge

in the searing unearthly wind.

THE ONE WHO SKINS CATS

She never liked to stay or live where she could not see the mountains, for home she called them. For the unseen spirit dwelt in the hills, and a swift-running creek could preach a better sermon for her than any mortal could have done. Every morning she thanked the spirits for a new day.

She worshipped the white flowers that grew at the snowline on the sides of the tall mountains. She sometimes believed, she said, that they were the spirits of little children who had gone away but who returned every spring to gladden the pathway of those now living.

I was only a boy then but those words sank deep down in my soul. I believed them then, and I believe now that if there is a hereafter, the good Indian's name will be on the right side of the ledger. Sacagawea is gone—but she will never be forgotten.

—Tom Rivington

1.

Sacagawea, Bird Woman

Bird Woman they call me
for I am the wind.
I am legend. I am history.
I come and I go. My tracks
are washed away in certain places.
I am Chief Woman, Porivo. I brought
the Sundance to my Shoshoni people—I am
grandmother of the Sun.
I am the one who wanders, the one
who speaks, the one who watches,
the one who does not wait,
the one who teaches, the one who goes
to see, the one who wears a silver
medallion inscribed with the face
of a President. I am the one who
holds my son close within my arms,
the one who marries, the one
who is enslaved, the one who is beaten,
the one who weeps, the one who knows

14

the way, who beckons, who knows the wilderness.
I am the woman who knows the pass and where
the wild food waits to be drawn from the mother's breast.
I am the one who meets,
the one who runs away.
I am Slave Woman, Lost Woman, Grass Woman, Bird Woman.
I am Wind Water Woman and White Water Woman, and I come
and go as I please. And the club-footed man
who shelters me is Goat Man, is my son,
is the one who buried me
in the white cemetery so you would not forget me.
He took my worth to his grave
for the spirit people to eat.
I am Many Tongue Woman, Sacred Wind Woman,
Bird Woman. I am Mountain Pass
and River Woman. I am free.
I know many places, many things.
I know enough to hear the voice
in the running water of the creek,
in the wind, in the sweet, tiny flowers.

2.

Porivo, Chief Woman

Yeah. Sure. Chief Woman, that's
what I was called. Bird Woman. Snake
Woman. Among other things. I've had
a lot of names in my time. None of em
fit me very well, but none of em was
my true name anyway,
so what's the difference?

Those white women who decided I alone
guided the whiteman's expedition across
the world. What did they know?
Indian maid, they said.
Maid. That's me.

But I did pretty good for a maid.
I went wherever I pleased, and
the whiteman paid the way.
I was worth something then.   I still am.
But not what they say.

There's more than one way
to skin a cat.   That's what they say
and it makes me laugh.   Imagine me,
Bird Woman, skinning a cat.
I did a lot of skinning in my day.

I lived a hundred years or more
but not long enough to see the day
when those white women, suffragettes,
made me the most famous squaw in all creation.
Me.   Snake Woman.   Chief.
You know why they did that?
Because they was tired of being nothing
themselves.   They wanted to show how nothing
was really something of worth.
And that was me.   Indian squaw,
pointing the way they wanted to go.
Indian maid, showing them how they oughta be.
What Susan B. Anthony had to say
was exactly right: they couldn't have
made it without me.

Even while I was alive, I was worth something.
I carried the proof of it in my wallet
all those years.   They saw how I rode the train
all over the West for free.   And how I got
food from the white folks along the way.
I had papers that said I was Sacagawea,
and a silver medal the President had made for me.

But that's water under the bridge.
I can't complain,

even now when so many of my own kind
call me names. Say
I betrayed the Indians
into the whiteman's hand.
They have a point,
but only one.
There's more than one way to skin a cat,
is what I always say.

One time I went wandering—
that was years after the first trip west,
long after I'd seen the ocean and the whale.
Do you know my people laughed
when I told em about the whale?
Said I lied a lot.
Said I put on airs.
Well, what else should a Bird Woman wear?

But that time I went wandering out West.
I left St. Louis because my squawman, Charbonneau,
beat me. Whipped me so I couldn't walk.
It wasn't the first time, but that time I left.
Took me two days to get back on my feet
Then I walked all the way to Comanche country
in Oklahoma, Indian Territory it was then.
I married a Comanche man, a real husband,
one I loved. I stayed there nearly 27 years.
I would have stayed there till I died,
but he died first.

After that I went away. Left the kids,
all but one girl I took with me but
she died along the way—not as strong
as she should be, I guess. But
the others, they was Comanche after all,
and I was nothing, nothing at all.
Free as a bird. That's me.

That time I went all the way
to see the Apaches, the Havasupai,
all sorts of Indians. I wanted
to see how they were faring. I like
the Apaches, they were good to me.
But I wouldn't stay long. I had fish to fry.
Big ones. Big as the whales
they said I didn't see.

Oh, I probably betrayed some Indians.
But I took care of my own Shoshonis.
That's what a Chief Woman does, anyway.
And the things my Indian people call me now
they got from the whiteman, or, I should say,
the white women. Because it's them who said
I led the whitemen into the wilderness and back,
and they survived the journey with my care.
It's true they came like barbarian hordes
after that, and that the Indian lost our place.
We was losing it anyway.

I didn't lead the whitemen, you know. I just
went along for the ride. And along the way
I learned what a chief should know,
and because I did, my own Snake people survived.
But that's another story,
one I'll tell some other time.
This one's about my feathered past,
my silver medallion I used to wear to buy my rides
to see where the people lived, waiting for
the end of the world.

And what I learned I used. Every bit
of the whiteman's pride to make sure
my Shoshoni people would survive
in the great survival sweepstakes of the day.
Maybe there was a better way to skin that cat,

but I used the blade that was put in my hand—
or my claw, I should say.

Anyway, what it all comes down to is this:
The story of Sacagawea, Indian maid,
can be told a lot of different ways.
I can be the guide, the chief.
I can be the traitor, the Snake.
I can be the feathers on the wind.
It's not easy skinning cats
when you're a dead woman.
A small brown bird.

IROQUOIS SUNDAY: WATERTOWN, 1982

"If it doesn't make awareness higher,
it isn't art," he said, that Indian
from Ottowa. He'd come all the way
for the powwow. To sell some pictures
and carvings he'd made. "You see
the serpent, the woman, the man. You know
what Freud says about serpents," he said
to my white friend, staring at her the way
men do at women. She knew. Moved uneasy,
angry, away. She told me about it
later, after we left and went to the
Dairy Queen in town for a bite to eat.
He'd shown us his pictures, discoursing
on the nature of true art. One of them
was of two tree stumps that had a few
branches rising slender toward the sky.
If you looked at it just right you could see
an eagle hovering, wings pointed down,
over two heads, the man's looking up and out,
the woman's lowered, humbly behind. He
pointed that out, or you wouldn't have known
one was a man's, one was a woman's.

"What kind of Indian are you?" I asked.
He didn't say, but I know. Coyote Indian.
There was a big stone grinding wheel
mounted on a stand. The children played
with it all afternoon. The powwow was at
one of the women's houses
that was built on a suburban plot.
It was made of logs. Sitting
on the front steps, we watched the clouds.
The children tumbled in the grass like raccoons.
When it began to rain, everyone went inside.
Sat around, talking, watching the children
play. The men wandered from room to room.

They played poker with the Tarot cards.
The women watched the corn soup boiling,
the coffee dripping into the pyrex pot,
the hot scones browning. Those women
don't talk to eagles. They talk to snakes.
To the grandmothers. They tell fortunes
with the cards. They read omens
beneath the sky. They count raindrops
in time to every latest craze. They survive,
grinding axes, teeth, fingers and minds
sharp as blades.

TAKING A VISITOR TO SEE THE RUINS

for Joe Bruchac

He's still telling about the time he came west
and was visiting me. I knew he
wanted to see some of the things

everybody sees when they're in the wilds of New Mexico.
So when we'd had our morning coffee
after he'd arrived, I said,

Would you like to go see some old Indian ruins?
His eyes brightened with excitement,
he was thinking, no doubt,

of places like the ones he'd known where he came from,
sacred caves filled with falseface masks,
ruins long abandoned, built secure

into the sacred lands; or of pueblos
once home to vanished people but peopled still
by their ghosts, connected still with the bone-old land.

Sure, he said. I'd like that a lot.
Come on, I said, and we got in my car,
drove a few blocks east, toward the towering peaks

of the Sandias. We stopped at a tall
high-security apartment building made of stone,
went up a walk past the pond and pressed the buzzer.

They answered and we went in,
past the empty pool room, past the empty party room,
up five flights in the elevator, down the abandoned hall.

Joe, I said when we'd gotten inside the chic apartment,
I'd like you to meet the old Indian ruins
I promised.

My mother, Mrs. Francis, and my grandmother, Mrs. Gottlieb.
His eyes grew large, and then he laughed
looking shocked at the two

women he'd just met. Silent for a second, they laughed too.
And he's still telling the tale of the old
Indian ruins he visited in New Mexico,

the two who still live pueblo style in high-security dwellings
way up there where the enemy can't reach them
just like in the olden times.

TWO

Heyoka, Coyote Tales
Songs of Colonization

HORNS OF A DILEMMA

any bird that wants to fly has two wings.
any beast that wants to walk has four legs.
or two. or six. or eight.
fish have tails that sail them
left and right. so they can get through the water.

people have one brain. they use it to think
one way. they don't get anywhere. they don't
go anywhere. they stay put.
some people.

others have brains with two sides and three parts
and twenty million cells and unnumbered fluids
made of uncountable proportions of multitudinous
substances. all are used. accounted for.

the people of one brain
use it to shame the other brain.
they say they are shaming whatever
is not themselves. they don't know
the other is the other side of one.
they don't know that there never was one side.

a bird born with one wing can't fly.
what's that poor bird to do?
the bird with one wing will die.
why do the birds let that happen?
because they're cruel.
because they're indifferent.
because they're powermad.
because they lack compassion.
because they're stupid. dumb birds.
(we are smarter and better than birds.
we people wouldn't let a onewinged bird die.)
but the birds say that a onewinged bird can't fly.

once i met a fish who refused
to use her tail like other fish did.

why should the right side get the same play
as the left side, she said. the right side
gets all the attention. i won't move my tail
from side to side. i will only wave it on the left
side. that fish died.

the Hopi say that the twohorn gods
are the wisest and eldest gods. they're so old
they use both sides to see from. what they see
is so true that they don't try to say it.
the onehorn people couldn't understand.
the twohorn gods participate in things the
rest do, but they will not be responsible
for the consequences of partial vision.

FANTASIA REVOLUTION

We had dreams
about the crystal sun
the juniper wind, apple
blossoms and glowing evenings
comfort and quietude

we had dreams
lollipops and no one crying
no pain—and love if not
everlasting
solid and smiling every day

we had dreams
about great ships sailing
wind filling all speed ahead
never becalmed, no one dead,
no rotting bodies on the deck
no witness to inexplicable agony

we had dreams
garlands from gardens
nobody had to tend
ice cream cones piling
sidewalks high
shade for the asking
from every uncomfortable
ray of sun
water enough for everything
lawns and trees
flowers and livestock
children running in sprinklers
water for the taking
every day

we had dreams
soft conversations in
the lamplight, hands to hold
slim and strong whenever

we needed, voices filled
with understanding and strength
for every fear
and every tear dried
by gentle caring touch

we had dreams
that did not include random bullets
sudden death and no clouds
exploding to rain death
on helpless heads

we dreamed we would never be helpless
we had dreams
we bought on time
amortization forever
and no one would ever
have to pay the bills

we had dreams
someone would always save us
mother always did
even when she didn't want to
even when we made her mad
even when we broke her china
and her heart

we had dreams
laughing and crying
talking into loudspeakers
shouting our claims
and never thought how
to make them come true

we had dreams
of glory and taking
down every flag from every
highest hill

and no one would be found
face down in two inches of water
drowned on booze and disaster

we had dreams
that did not include spit
on the sidewalk, in the gutters,
but only clean skies
and apple pie, organically sweet
every day
and endlessly billowing
wheat, and sailing ships
and all the pure water
we could drink for free
and play in

we had dreams
that we could demand pain away
and guilt and the necessary consequences
of our dreams that mothers would pay
if we dreamed hard enough
and played hard enough
and the nasty old piper
never called for his fee

we had dreams
and when they didn't come true
we had curses

we cursed the lollipops
we cursed the ice cream
we cursed the wheat
the cornucopia
the great sailing ships
and the sea
the mother
the sidewalks
the highest hills

and the trickling ditch
we cursed the livestock
and the stereos
the loudspeakers and the glory
and we cursed crying and apple pie
we cursed suffering and anguish
the pipers who demanded to be paid
the ones who paid and complained
about the mess we made
we cursed fine china plates
filled with hard-earned harvests
we cursed love and freedom
we cursed crystal sun
and shade.

YESTERDAY'S CHILD

as I awake, I find me lying,
arm flung beyond the pine bed's
varnished gloss confine,
tears streaming, mouth open—
for breath? for speaking?
and hear me saying in the tangle of my mind
I want my son. I want Gene.

I had been dreaming about him,
the twenty-three-year-old man who is my son,
not about him, really, but about talking
with some woman about him. she was telling me
that I needed to trust, to know he was safe
doing what men do—going about his business.
she was blond with very short tight-curled hair,
teeth broken or chipped, somewhat older than me.

waking, I don't know who she is
or how in the world I could see Gene
who is so far away from me. it was as though
she had a crystal ball, or a closed-circuit t.v.
but only in the mind—I'm not sure whether it was
hers or mine or one we shared
—but I could see him for myself,
see that what she told me was the truth.

still, waking,
finding old tears wet on me,
arm flung barely beyond the limit of my sleep,
understanding stretched
just armslength into the unknown space
the stranger-woman opened up to me,
I remember I am a mother.
I want to see Gene, to talk to him out loud,
see for myself that he's all right,
know whether he has grown
more hair, a mustache, a beard,

find out what he's been thinking about,
who he lives with now, whether
he's working, eating, staying away
from dope and booze and dirty air

as I get up I find me angry
at the vanished son who does not call

COYOTE JUNGLE

The man across from me
sits tight, holding
together all the plans
of another time,
pointed toe edging
cautious toward a future
of electronic landscape.
Even the forests
have been wired, plugged in
to terminals far away.
He doesn't understand
that the furrow on his
forehead was transferred
from the furrows he once turned
on the land, embedded there
by lightning flash that stunned
him, knocked him silly
as he sat on the tractor
waiting out Nebraska storm.
On that day,
Earth marked him as her own,
and blinded by that light
to tractor hum and rich,
new-turned clods,
he walked to town
carrying nothing but a small
squat black box for doctoring
and a stranger's way of knowing.
Now he sits near me,
squinting into the velvet dark
of technological truth,
muttering with vanished wizards:

DO WHAT THOU WILT
SHALL BE THE WHOLE OF THE LAW

and there casts the enchantment
that will frame our lives anew.
He does not comprehend
the fire-studded darkness
of the words that fall: *silver,*
camphor, mercury, copper, gold,
iron, brass and *lead,* ancient
ritual revitalized on smog-
heavy mountain air.
Jeremiah in the wild,
Coyote hunched on the north-
east border of urban sprawl
he grows sheep and doctors
broken pets;
he builds strong fences
to cradle baby and wife in,
he speaks words to banish
terror in face of the dark
he knows he is facing:
goddam coyotes,
I'd like to see em raise em
in the cities, like
em to see the gutted bellies
of the lambs those varmints
leave behind.

TEACHING POETRY AT VOTECH HIGH, SANTA FE, THE WEEK JOHN LENNON WAS SHOT

I

Crepe paper Christmas,
green and red, turns
and twists, symmetrical,
around the partitioned
segments of the barnsized room—
voices of brown and white young,
rejects from more hallowed halls
on their way to factories in some
nameless and partitioned open space
in the unbending world
of their faceless fate—blend with
mechanical and electronic chatter.
Noise everywhere, scrambling over
untouched books glossy and slick
with disuse. A groan and clatter
of highmigraine screech pulses
unidentified, predictable,
sets my teeth on edge.
My brainends turn, twist,
try to tune themselves
to unpredictability,
to something textured,
recognizable. Still,
I inhabit this slick universe:
hired to teach glossy poetry.
Through their eyes,
I see myself punitive, demanding, irrelevant.
Though I am not
vocationally authorized,
I hold the chalk.

Electronic mornings creep
over my horizon,
fill my days with danger, hang

ominous over the Rio Grande,
chase the mesas north.
On the highway early
driving north from Albuquerque
I saw sunrise gold and dayglopink billow
on the smoke of the electric plant
outside of Bernalillo.
So much beauty in the certain destruction
it spewed into the December crystal air.
Winter settling on the land, a nestling bird.
Stalks of winter-frosted grass
pointed to me my way, made
my pathway clear.
Last night on the late news
they announced John Lennon's murder,
said he died climbing the stairs.
Remembering when I
was on the other side of the desk,
the twenty years between,
I wept.
How had we come to this?
The shots that took him down
spewed a strawberry trail on the steps,
the blood washed away just after
by the city's rain.

II

The best of the world
slumps before me in the room—
minds that eighteen years ago
first turned earthward blinking:
oh yeah.
Wasted.
Turned off.
Tuned in to video narcosis,
stereophonic shuddering light,

in which, transfixed,
these naked angels burn golden pink,
their hopes and mine on dust and booze.
They smirk about "Ever Clear,"
explain when I ask
that it's 180 proof alcohol
unaware of the implications in the name,
of what
another time
the words might mean—
or perhaps not unaware.
There is a certain glint
on each institution-frosted face.
They have grown,
unawares, into electronic commodities,
haven't the will to fight
the mindless nothing that infuses
inexorable anguish into their lives.
Stoned like martyrs of their ancient faith
they go down their days
not understanding
how they've been crucified,
or by who,
they make do with plastic reveries sunk
in heedless desperation.
Synthetic clatter crusts
their days, makes electro-
chemical tissue of their gaze.

What world is this?
Cut off, torn away, shattered, maybe
they dream of when it will get better,
of when they will be free.

III

180 proof.

Neither womb nor honest texture provides
rough comfort or sure throbbing grasp.
Quivering, these desperados
hide beneath sham and sneer,
behind closed eyes, disheveled hair,
stoned on chemicals and beer.
What do they become, these children,
the same age as my own,
who I watch staggering into life,
despair rising
brown and stinking within their eyes
like poison on the desert air?
It billows gold and pink
around their faces, their helpless heads:
They do not plan, they do not dream.
There is no future they can bear.
I want to cradle them,
murmur to keep them from knowing
what I fear.
I will not let them see me weep.
I will fight with them instead,
sneer and rage.
Tell them to be quiet, to sit down.

IV

No munchkin voices. An English
sharpwood point breaks with a smug tap.
Muffled sounds rise in my ears,
the bite of lemon fills my nostrils.
They pass it around, juice sticking
to their hands. I am surrounded
by eyes that canny and closed
measure me, gaze surreptitiously
from faces no more than
nineteen years old.

Artificiality-induced
boredom barely masks
their scorn of the dusty
plastic tiempo their minds are frozen in;
barely differentiated into carpets,
chalkboards, partitions,
desks, shelves, jackets, slacks,
glossy animal posters on the walls.
They understand
the nature of their punishment.
They do not understand their crimes.
They sit behind plastic faces
barely differentiated into closed
and empty, resentful and dazed. They
are sick with disuse,
plasticized in atrophic rage.

V

Touch skin:
one's own
dewy with petrochemicals
soft for now.
Remember wood
gleaming and warm
accepting you—
smells and oils,
polishing.
Handle plastic
that refuses to recognize
whatever it is you are,
huddled into petrochemical clothing
acrylic
cold
unrewarding
no energy in it.

Know the exact dimension
of a dying soul.

VI

Tired.
Week nearly done.
Mind a tree,
peeling dead bark
littering the ground,
waiting
for the last molecule
to be released.
This rubble of ash
shaped into glazed and battered blocks
forms the walls, grey because they are
held together by despair.
Roughshod voices ride
the lockerlined metalclanging corridor.
Eyes glitter on the brink
of suicide.
The principal stalks the lateday halls
the tiny snackbar beyond the farther door.
He collars those who loiter
in these dispirited halls,
haranguing, ordering. His brown face
looks siempre tired.
His familiar Chicano body sags slightly
into his next word. He knows
what he sees. His limp loose tie
bespeaks discouragement, fatigue.
The students allow his harsh
ministrations, pretend to obey
until he is out of sight down the hall,
then return to loitering,
neck halfheartedly, play pinball

on a slightly sagging machine.
Two o'clock.
Ten more minutes and I'll be free.

I teach the students lost
to plastic rugs and desks,
watch silty minds
grainy to my touch's thought,
ooze helpless to the glazed acrylic floor.
Before me one young face
reflected in hand-held glass
gleams.

VII

Wood steel over emotional motivation sullen
firetaste smoke harsh hash herbs gross green
bitter lemonpeel coffeegrounds awful seeds
like wood burning nutcrust walnutskin goats
milk the aftertaste liquidy resin kumquats
sour cherries sharp a tar burn tongues fire
stream chill flight harpoon spiraling tight
grapefruit tangy bite spaced torn from shoots
green apricots sour blackberries grogged air
kind of asleep stomach hurt chest sorry full
tingle muscle pulse pulse pulse speed to
flight adrer.alin spike taking off meadows rise
in pleasuring thick as sour cream rancid cheese
fresh milk from fat dusty cows taste of blood
coats warm throat what do we do with the hole
thats left staggering bleeding on the steps
ripe ripped on the powered air stale burning
rising incense nicotine sweet fingers nauseous
air content powdered sugar hills stiff grass
pointing billowing into blood the pain a mom
ent only gone fish ride lakes na'more clear
defined strawberry place rising a stair plas

tic fields silent   time grows in cement cracks
soft fiber fall   a feather of breath   lemon air

VIII

Around me
the faces are forests
retreating into snow they
whisper about taking her down
giggle defiance . eyes
prepared for punishment
because they KNOW, in carnality
(¡oigan! ¡carnales!)
My words fall on history-reddened ears
She? / He? Who is it that speaks?
"See, man—I mean ma'am (smirk)
You know HE'S talking to HER
because the Beatles are male, man,
and HE says:
let me take you down"
(leering at the thought).
(Dying at the shot, yeah, man,
he's been taken down, *verdad*.)
They do not mention the tone of grief.

Winter here. We wish for spring.
For ease maybe somewhere
for running across fields
forever alive forever free
in some packaged plastic freeze-
dried recurrent fantasy.
But red with the ridicule of self-abuse
in front of me their postures are
vaguely fused to the carmine blaze of rage
that right to the quick bites deep,
touches me in that secret place
where no one dares to go, not even me,

though I KNOW
that inward lifelong sentence, that
single thought that holds
a life in matter's field,
that now bruised and icy bleeds
sweet juice red as ripe berries
on the forever frozen grass

IX

The noise and clutter
of each separate day
fuses into sound:
learned in grit
in multidecible shriek, we
learned to say what there is to say
under bricks, under rubble of dead
elephants' dream
transformed into heaps of ivory
hedge against inflation
learned that daddy won't come home

he was never there anyway
to take it step by step
like one child stepped
(how many years ago)
trying to get home
scrambling among words
groping for comprehension
among the sneers alongside the tears,
cut off in the smoke of winter air—
a life and a not necessary death
sufficient for that time—still, quiet, dead.

Later that day it rained.

TAKU SKANSKAN

that history is an event
that life is
that I am event
ually going to do something
the metaphor for god.
eventuality.
activity.

what happens *to be*
what happens *to me*
god. history. action
the Lakota word for it is:
whatmovesmoves.
they don't call god "what moves something."
not "prime mover."
"first mover" "who moves everything or nothing."
"action." "lights." "movement."
not "where" or "what" or "how" but
event.   GOD
is what happens, is:
movesmoves.

riding a mare.
eventuality.
out of the corral into morning
taking her saddled and bridled
air thick with breath movesmoves
horsebreath, mybreath, earthbreath
skybreathing air. ing.
breathesbreathes movesmoves
in the cold. winterspringfall.
corral. ing. horse and breath.
air. through the gate moveswe.
lift we the wooden crossbar *niya*
movesmoves unlocks movesbreathes
lifebreath of winter soul
swings wide sweet corral gate

happens to be frozenstiff in place
happens to be cold. so I and mare
wear clothes thatmove in event
of frozen. shaggydressers for the air that
breathes breathe we: flows: movesmoves:
god its cold.
no other place but movemove
horse me gate hinge air bright frost lungs burst
swing gate far morning winter air rides
movesmovingmoves Lakotas say: god.
what we do.

THREE

Naku, Woman
Songs of Generation

WHAT THE MOON SAID

The moon lives in all the alone places
all alone.
    "There are things
    I work out for myself," she says.
    "You don't have to be depressed about them.
    These are my paces, and walking through them
                             is my right.
    You don't need to care
                when I'm down.

    "Or if I'm mad at myself, don't believe
                       I'm mad at you.
    If I glare it is not your face I am staring at
                    but my own.
    If I weep, it is not your tears that flow.

   "And if I glow
    with the brush of twilight wings,
    if I rise round and warm
             above your bed,
    if I sail
         through the iridescent
                autumn spaces
  heavy with promise,
              with red and fruity light,
  and leave your breath
             tangled in the tossing tops
  of trees as I arise,
  as I speed away into the far distance,
  disappearing as you gaze,
  turning silver, turning white,
  it is not your glory I reflect.
  It is not your love
     that makes me pink,
                 copper,
                    gold.
It is mine."

The moon moves along the sky by her own willing.
It is her nature to shed some light, sometimes
to be full and close, heavy with unborn thought
on rising. It is her nature sometimes
to wander in some distant place, hidden, absent, gone.

AROUSINGS

1.

clear the ditch
the roadway.
get them freed and long,
walk alongside them watch
water running
clear and frothy, cold.
let the rain
in through the pores
let it wash clear the pane,
let the air in, break
the glass, stay within the bounds
of reason, loading up with things
lovely and necessary, things
that are dry, things that are lost.
go away from meaning into longing.
go far and long, go wide, go deep, go on.
let the craft go on pitching
on the highhigh waves,
let it cast the winds away, let
the rain go down the face, the trunk,
the body's limbs, let it roar and tumble,
let the wind wash clear
the dire spaces, all disease,
the tall twisted places of the dark,
the roman arches, the goths and visigoths,
the slaughter.
let the water drench with laughter,
with what there is that's cool,
with what there is that's sweet.
at Laguna in the proper season
they clean the ditches.
so life bearer will freely pour.
they call it wonder.
water.
they call it thought.
they call it peaceful hearts

and sharing. caring. caring for.

2.

across the emptiness of grey
spray of rain on the highway
becoming your face,
across the moisture-laden miles
the hills pouring with her sweat
her grateful tears of release,
recognition, recognized
see her, how she rises
her breath frothy deep on the air,
her gasping, her need:
she has a new lover this year.
have you noticed how wet
she's becoming, how erratic?
she smiles and roars,
pours in perfect passion,
tosses her hair, body,
her legs,
she claps her hands, she sings.
she dances.
the grandlady, so fine this year,
this season, this solstice, this
solace, this spring.
and your eyes grey reflect her joy
they glow like miles at sea, like rising
fog. i think of her touch,
your hands
subtle and quick.
i think of small furry creatures, ferret, raccoon.
of how you spit and hissed the first year through,
how you bit me then:
tiny sharp teeth baring
so lately let free from the cage
of mortality. of your fear.

i think of how you loved
desperately.

3.

how you loved me. made love to me.
what i saw there when i was held.
in the wild tangle of our tongues' necessity,
rooting in softleafed places,
melting and pouring like the hills today,
ground gone to water, running toward the sea,
heat rising but not in rage.
in love.
just the seagrey of your gaze,
your longing, arms raised to clasp
me,
    in sight
            of the Woman
        she
            lying in a pond
                        in the woods
            in the pond of her self,
                        her dreams.
        lying breathless, she.
        taken with a dream
        a sighting
        of her lovely lover
                who is coming down,
                            running, down
        to meet her where she's waiting
        in her pond, in her lake, in her sea.
    we could see her waiting
                for the time to be
                            her time.
        her arms ready to rise
        her knees beginning to open, to lift,

we said: she's waking to love.
after so long a time
the sleeping one awakens.
what will that mean?
looking into each other's eyes,
the question spun between us,
glimmered in the softlight,
thoughts, butterflies, moths, soft wings dipping
between our lips, our eyes:

                    know this:
          the woman of the earth.
          the woman of the sky.
          the woman of the water,
          of the seaspray.
          the fog.
          wakes.

will pour down
                    in the mountain soil.
will descend
                    on the limbs of fallen trees.
will blow free
               in the sleet,
                         the blizzard winds
wrapped in white as becomes one just awakened.

          the woman of the hives, of the bees;
          the woman of the cocoon, the butterflies;
          the woman of the coiling meanders, the time
          the woman of the snaking fires, the flame
          the woman of the water, the snow, the rain.

the woman whose waking means
wonder.
water.
want and need.
and her awakening is not death or war, not rage.
she's in love, that woman the world. she's in love.

SOMETHING FRAGILE, BROKEN

1.

i had seen something
i had wanted

and sorrow is not to enter
into it:

a sparrow falling: a tiny
fragile egg, crushed

it was in the grass then
fallen, dead.

reached out, that hand,
palm open, such care

fallen anyway, all the way
to the ground

where it smashed.
the slate stones that ringed

the lily pond of my grandmother
held it, blue and broken.

sorrow was not to enter
into it. but it did.

and i am not stone but shell,
blue and fragile. dropped,

i splatter. spill the light
all over the stone

nothing that can be mended.

2.

sorrow was not to enter this

but it did. and i
was not to weep, or

think such things or
let you see that this,

which was not to be entered,
was born and broken before

entering. not in tears
exactly, not fallen in

that way, but still.
and i knew what would not

be spoken. a circle that
would not be broken

shattered anyway, or died.
like ripples on the lake,

when the stone has sunk
deep beneath the surface,

die. sorrow has no part
in it. some things just

don't go on. some circles
come undone. some sparrows

fall. sometimes sorrow,
in spite of resolution,

enters in.

DEAR WORLD

Mother has lupus.
She says it's a disease
of self-attack.
It's like a mugger broke into your home
and you called the police
and when they came they beat up on you
instead of on your attackers,
she says.

I say that makes sense.
It's in the blood,
in the dynamic.
A halfbreed woman
can hardly do anything else
but attack herself,
her blood attacks itself.
There are historical reasons
for this.

I know you can't make peace
being Indian and white.
They cancel each other out.
Leaving no one in the place.
And somebody's gotta be there,
to take care of the house,
to provide the food.
And that's gotta be the mother.
But if she's gone to war.
If she's beaten and robbed.
If she's attacked by everyone.
Conquered, occupied, destroyed
by her own blood's diverse strains,
its conflicting stains?

Well, world. What's to be done?
We just wait and see
what will happen next.

The old ways go,
tormented in the fires of disease.
My mother's eyes burn,
they tear themselves apart.
Her skin darkens in her fire's heat,
her joints swell to the point
of explosion, eruption.
And oh, the ache: her lungs
don't want to take in more air,
refuse further oxygenation:
in such circumstances,
when volatile substances are intertwined,
when irreconcilable opposites meet,
the crucible and its contents vaporize.

WEED

She stood, a weed tall in the sun.
She grew like that and went
over it again and again trying to be tall
trying not to die in the drying sun
the seeming turbulence of waiting
the sun so yellow
so still

There was nothing else to do. It was like that
in her day, and the sun who rose so bright
so full of fire reminded her of that.
It was the sun that did it; it was the rain.
She stood it all, and more:
the water pounding from the high rock face
of the mesas that made her yard
she knew where she was growing. Didn't
she know what sun will do, what happens to weeds
when their growing time's done? Didn't she care?
She got the sun into her, though.
The fire. She drank the rain for fuel.
She stood there in the day, growing,
trying to stand tall like a right weed would.

The drying was part of it.
The dying. Come from heat, the transformation
of fire. The rain helped because it understood
why she just stood there, growing,
tall in the heat and bright.

MYTH/TELLING - DREAM/SHOWING

1.

so where do we go next?
(into sunrise)

2.

there is all the clutter:
on the walls, the table top,
in the sink, all over the counters,
on the stove, the sofa, the floors.

3.

the bird, yellow, green and blue
who lives in a cage with an open door
chirps now and then. drops onto the table
for breakfast.

4.

the cloud in the north, she said.
she meant the united states.

5.

I don't care, he said. I love
the united states. it isn't fair.
I never killed any indians. I am not
responsible for what my ancestors did.
I love the wilderness, he said. the indians
can't keep me out of it.

6.

and then there's the indian woman
who hates in herself what is white.
says she sees it like vomit. like
a crippled withered leg she must drag
with her everywhere she goes.

7.

and there is all the litter. the hours
passing. the exhaustion. the cloud
that is what I have to do today. not
go to the water. not go to the mesa.
go into the city. the cloud.

8.

the indian woman is cursed with lupus.
a blood disease. in which your blood
devours you.

9.

the white man goes to yosemite
on vacation. it's his recreation.
yes, says another man, black. it's
your recreation, but it's their life.

10.

the north of here is oregon, washington.
mt. st. helen's. that cloud.

11.

the bird dreams in his cage.
about lunch. he doesn't dream of trees.
he never saw one, doesn't know what they are.

12.

I have to put my feathers on.
go through the door that opens.
into wilderness. city traffic.
bird-empty streets.

13.

if dawn comes (if corn comes).
if it is sunrise. that soft and blessing.
where someone is going, next.
if spring comes. (summer-people time.)
corn-is-growing time.
where/when-someone-is-going-next time.

GRANDMA'S DYING POEM

for Aggie

When somebody dies
you have to consider.
When the last grandmother dies
you have to reflect.

She's somehow what your life has been
all along,
you realize—your life has been
a mirror of her ways, the reflection
slightly different by small changes
time and fashion make. When
her place is empty, do you move in?
Do you take her barking staccato
voice that modulates in a different key
to say what can be said (as so much can't)?
Do you forget, did she ever know to the bone
the delicacy of porcelain as her skin,
or seductive fall of lash,
beguiling coif to frame her face
the perilous fragility of lace
clasped fine with cameo
to grace a slender elegant length of neck
that was her own?
No, not for her a light fluting voice
or feminine coy
glance to pass down to me—
I could never step graceful
to frail dance any more than she
(though she might deny); the speed of Virginny Reel,
Corn Dance and Seboyeta Waltz were more our style—
But didn't she try? How she tried.

I wonder, grandma. I look
at your 18-year-old face
gazing steady out at me

from an 83-year-old photograph,
eyes softened by some photographer's ploy, fine
hair done smooth and plain
over turn-of-the-century rats
except for those fly-away wisps
you never could control
your soft hair, thicker then,
nearly gone by the time you died.
Hairiness not any part of your line, grandma,
not on any side:
no raven Indian princess locks to hang thick heavy
down your back, no graceful elegance of white
that ladies in your century's books wore like a crown
(or mine).

So what are we, if not the ladies
as you so long supposed? Or did you know?
Ladies don't look directly,
don't bark their words,
are not abrupt, determined,
demanding like you, like me. So
I am undone by the nature of genetic lines—
Or is it the force of learning, strong,
of knowing you all my life? After all
I grew up next door to you,
saw you every day my first seven years
before I went away to school,
and often enough afterward.
Surely I would have learned
from all that, grandma, how to be
a wanderer in an alien land,
a pretender to customs I cannot claim
just as I learned to listen for your breath
while I lay next to you not so long ago,
where we rested
safe in my mother's,
your daughter's house,

wondering if you slept
or simply waited,
like you waited all the long dark
days after you lost your sight,
your power to move and shape and hold,
your house, your garden, your music,
your soul, your life.
In those days you spent stalking your death
I wondered what you thought through
those obscure hours day and night,
what you waited for.
What fire burned in you?
(And it was a fire, I know.)

I think now about the ways I knew you:
presiding over a kitchen's clicking toaster,
butane stove those so many years ago,
burning trash in the rust-red barrel,
burning breakfast napkins in the iron kitchen stove,
heaping coal into the dark
iron hole that kept us warm.
Or bending in your summer yard
over a tidy riot of flowers,
ever threatened by mutiny of weeds,
head held sturdy under broad straw hat
cotton shirt and slacks kept from grime
by a loose flowing smock
—or do I imagine that?
Didn't I see (how often)
you drag and whip miles of heavy hose to pour
precious desert water over mulched acres of dirt
until you could make them yield
to your tenacious pinto terrier will?
I would have learned from that, grandma, I suppose.
That would be something I wouldn't forget, unless
I know your being because it is my own.
(But didn't you cry? How I cried.)

Another thing that won't erase—
the howl of face you died with
the look neither soft nor serene—not composed,
the one that knew no gentling—and that unearthly
protesting wail of NOOOOOOOOOOOOOOO
to death—like an animal, my mother said—
the sound I didn't hear
but recognized from her account as mine
years before you came upon your death
as she stood by the couch
you lay on that last time
looking down on you in anguish, in fear—
a sound of monster wind, *chindi*, devil moan,
flung beyond betrayed, betraying breath,
wrung from you as you began to see
that some things can't be denied, turned down.
(Did you think death was a bed,
a stack of dirty dishes,
a stand of roses, petunias,
poppies, cats, dogs, children
you could bulldog to your will?)
Is there not a similar wind, moan, howl, will
in me—placed there by double helix,
their dance and spiral—RNA, DNA—or by
living beside you as I have all my life
until you died, and often enough afterward?
I still ache with desolation
in a similar wind.
(Grandma, what's it like to die?)

Do you suppose that
when grandma dies
more of her stays than goes?

SIGHTINGS I: MUSKOGEE TRADITION

Deer Woman comes so they say
Her beauty is entrancing
they don't mean metaphorically—
at stomp dance sometimes
She joins the dancers
in the awefull light;

She dances alongside a victim
who's sometimes a man
sometimes a girl
and holds her eyes
keeps her from looking down
so the deer's feet She can't change
won't give warning—

that's how She casts her spell,
and when it's in place
She moves with the victim
off the dance ground
into the night:
no one sees the girl again
no one saw her leave.

They say sometimes that girl comes back
years later
to leave a baby with her folks to raise
says she's been hooking in the city
since she went away—

or maybe years later some hunters
find human bones
up in the hills
somewhere out of the way.

SIGHTINGS II

Dancing alongside Her victim a time
She holds her eyes
as tight as chains
the bewitched feels as beauty,
as longing-assuaging love
helpless she cannot assess
her peril nor can she perceive
the carelessness of the beauty
she loves unless
she can look down,
can somehow splinter the spell
of the wondrous woman's gaze,
can see Her feet are
slender split hooves,
She a heartbreakingly lovely deer
if only she could look down—
break that enchantment spinning stare
she could break away.
Failing, the victim's bones
will someday be reclaimed
by her mourning family
or she will return once or twice perhaps
to drop off her infant to be raised by her kin.
She won't remember much, or care,
her soul stolen with her heart,
her body given to empty heat
of service on the streets,
the needle's numbing bite,
her empty eyes.

I danced with Deer Woman one fine night.
Made helpless by the enchantment of Her eyes.
Couldn't look down in time.

NEW BIRTH

1.

You never feel it
till it's over—
the relief
at having survived
and the new sun
rising calmly as ever
before your eyes. It's
morning.
And what you began
uncomprehending
as shaken still
you gaze around
at the wreckage—
carnage, destruction—
the bodies you must
lay to rest
the tears you must
let flow
the anguish of the long
long war
the birds that stunned at first
sing once more
the fresh damp wind
blowing lifeward once again
the trees

2.

bind up the wounds
dig the graves
light the fires
pitch the bodies into them
remember
the past, honor
it with your tears

healing as female rain
what you could not feel
attending now to need
to the singe of new life
flowing with new tears
grateful that the destruction
cleared away the useless
the senseless
the never-to-be-born
the stillborn
the walking dead
making clear
the way
for cleansing winds to blow